Marco Pozam

Sun Tzu on the Canudos War

Marco Pozam

Sun Tzu on the Canudos War

Wise and mistaken decisions in the four expeditions

ScienciaScripts

Cover image: www.ingimage.com

This book is a translation from the original published under ISBN 978-613-9-67319-3.

Publisher:
Sciencia Scripts
is a trademark of
Dodo Books Indian Ocean Ltd. and OmniScriptum S.R.L publishing group

120 High Road, East Finchley, London, N2 9ED, United Kingdom
Str. Armeneasca 28/1, office 1, Chisinau MD-2012, Republic of Moldova, Europe
Printed at: see last page
ISBN: 978-620-7-67901-0

Dedication

I dedicate this work to all those who have always encouraged and supported me, especially my wife Gisele. To my friends, who have contributed directly or indirectly to this work, whether in the military or not, but who understand the real meaning of the phrase:
"War is first and foremost an internal combat; it is in the soul of each soldier that the battle is won or lost."

Marco A. F. Pozam

PREFACE

"When ancients need a guide beyond their experience, I provide wisdom, which is now your role. To provide guidance in the present, using the memories of the past. Memories are not just about the past determining our future. You can change things, you can improve things. That's life." (THE GIVER, 2014).

By analyzing the decisions made by the Brazilian Army officers who took part in the Canudos War in the light of Sun Tzu's ancient recommendations in "The Art of War", this work aims to highlight the military aspects of the conflict, which contributed to the changes that occurred in the strategic, tactical and operational military thinking of the Brazilian Army's military leaders at the beginning of the 20th century.

The Canudos War, although known to all as a socio-political and religious movement, actually has other aspects unknown to the vast majority of the population, especially with regard to the actions of the Brazilian Army.

Despite widespread historical coverage, the vast majority only deal with the social issues of the conflict, relegating aspects that, although relevant, are unknown to the vast majority, such as the military aspects of the combat.

However, these military aspects are not always successful, and this paper seeks to present an analysis of the Canudos War, focusing on the actions of the Brazilian Army, demonstrating its historical relevance, and comparatively exploring the decisions and actions taken by the Brazilian Army troops when compared with the recommendations of the strategist Sun Tzu in his famous book "The Art of War".

In this way, this book analyzes the military strategies employed in the Canudos War, the human and material planning carried out, the pre-combat analyses, during the confrontation, and the results after each expedition carried out in the fight against the Arraial de Canudos, compared to what Sun Tzu recommends should have been done.

Sun Tzu and The Art of War

"Strategy without tactics is the slowest way to victory. Tactics without strategy is noise before defeat." The maxim, by Sun Tzu, is self-explanatory. O Chinese general understood, some 2,500 years ago, the importance of planning to make any initiative prosper: from wars to businesses. O Tzu's "advice", summarized, would be more or less: have an objective, base your strategy well, develop tactics and win - in life, in war and in business." (SANTACREU,2017).

Words convince, but example drags!

I remember that the first time I heard this phrase, I was still a young Brazilian Army officer at the start of my career and it seemed to me to be just another of the many ready-made phrases we use in the military.

I was very wrong!

Some time later I clearly understood the teaching of this very simple phrase, and today I am certain that it represents the purest expression of how to motivate multidisciplinary teams.

As the leader of a Marine platoon with 40 people, all between the ages of 18 and 30, with completely different life experiences, totally different levels of education, and completely antagonistic desires and problems, one of my main tasks was to pass on knowledge about the use of armored personnel carriers in attack and defense situations.

It didn't seem complex to me to talk about the theory and history of using armored vehicles, with successes and failures recorded in history, analyzing and explaining to this group the mistakes and the reasons for the victories, because everyone understood that there was only one common goal: to deliver a highly efficient and effective result.

How can we make them a highly motivated group for this delivery?

How can we be sure that when we carry out these same military actions in practice, and simulate the situations in troop exercises, there won't be unforeseen errors or interpretations that differ from the situations I had described in theory to my platoon?

What could go wrong and should be avoided?

The answer was simple.

As demonstrated in Edgar Dale's (1969) theories of learning, after two weeks we remember 10% of what we read; 20% of what we hear; 30% of what we see; 50% of what we see and hear; 70% of what we say; and we remember 90% of what we say and do!

Perhaps this was one of the greatest lessons I learned in the military: everything needs to be simulated on the basis of prior understanding, which mitigates risks and reduces errors to a minimum, and needs to be reviewed after execution in order to collect and share the lessons learned.

Just as in the theater artists rehearse to exhaustion to ensure the perfection of a line, or just as the Allied armies trained and simulated for years before landing in Normandy, this is the secret of the example that drags.

Don't just go to your team and tell them what to do.

First of all, set the scene and explain why the work is important.

Then explain what the objective of that work is for the business strategy, however small that activity seems to be.

Next, detail how the activity should be carried out and, most importantly, demonstrate how you would do the activity if it had been assigned to you.

Finally - and most importantly - get the person who has been given the task, or the team as a whole, to explain what they will be doing, and listen carefully before intervening or criticizing their interpretation.

I guarantee that you will often be surprised by some new points of view and the ideas that people produce when they work in multidisciplinary teams combining their life experiences.

Remember, as a leader you have to make the best decisions and not always have the best ideas. Often the best ideas come from words that convince and make others think, and above all they come from the example that people have experienced.

When was the last time you guided your team, questioned their understanding and demonstrated or simulated with them what should be done, before simply telling them to do it?

It seems, as we'll see below, that in Canudos all these teachings were left aside and, in particular, most of the soldiers involved in the conflict forgot or simply didn't know everything that Sun Tzu and his "The Art of War" advocated almost 2,500 years before the Canudos War broke out.

Making the best decisions quickly can be a matter of life and death for a military operation or even for a business, the difference is between choosing and applying calculated risk or inconsequence.

SUMMARY

INTRODUCTION

The Art of War" is a military treatise written almost 3,000 years ago by the Chinese general Sun Tzu, based on his tactical and operational experience, in which he consolidated links about strategy that are applicable to various areas of knowledge.

Since then, and throughout the centuries, these links have been used to guide leaders, not just, one might suppose, the military.

This would explain why the "science of the art of war" still preserves Sun Tzu's main recommendations today, especially with regard to the figure of the military leader and his main qualities: secrecy, dissimulation, cunning and surprise, even though the tactics and means used in waging war have changed a lot.

In "The Art of War", Sun Tzu states that in order to win a war, a military leader must avoid five basic defects: rashness, hesitation, irascibility, preoccupation with appearances and excessive complacency; he must also know the terrain, its geography and, even more so, the men, both those under his command and those under the command of the enemy.

When we analyze the decisions made during the Canudos War in the light of Sun Tzu's work, the subject of this article, we surprisingly realize that the aspects mentioned above were little or not explored by the military leaders of the Brazilian Army and, likewise, the need to evaluate the necessary forces was also ignored.

On this last point, Sun Tzu says:

In military art, and in the good command of troops, there are only two kinds of force. Their combinations, however, are unlimited. No one can encompass them. These forces interact. They resemble, in practice, a chain of interconnected operations, сото multiple rings, or сото a wheel in motion, which one knows neither where it begins nor where it ends. (SUN TZU, 2000, p. 52)

Thus, we draw from Sun Tzu's link that the necessary forces can be defined as the simple combination of direct forces - which lead the battles, fixing and distracting the enemy - with indirect forces used to consolidate the results, by bursting into the theater of operations with axes where they are not expected.

Sun Tzu's observations and recommendations are applicable to all conflicts and, in many cases, guide the resolution of problems because they are a set of metaphors that allow analysis of the strategies adopted, as well as the decisions that led to them and their consequences.

Despite the existence of a complex theory on the subject of "decision-making", very often (as is commonly said in infantry units) during war decisions are made "by seeing the whites of the enemy's eyes". This fact is corroborated by modern thinkers such as Clausewitz:

The theory of major operations (strategy, it's called) presents extraordinary difficulties, and it's fair to say that few people have clear ideas about the details - that is, ideas that logically derive from basic needs. Most men act by instinct and the amount of success they achieve depends on the amount of talent they were born with. (CLAUSEWITZ, 1984, p. 72).

Returning to our object of study, the Canudos War - which lasted from November 7, 1896 to October 5, 1897 - this paper aims to present a brief analysis of the conflict with an emphasis on the military aspects of the combat and the decisions made by its military leaders.

We also try to show that these decisions can be considered wise or mistaken when analyzed in the light of the ancient teachings of the strategist Sun Tzu.

At this point, it's important to note that although most of the analysis was based on Sun Tzu's work, it wasn't the only one we used, but also other authors who specialize in the themes of war, such as Clausewitz.

We chose to look at the military aspects of the Canudos War based on Sun Tzu's work because the vast majority of recent works deal only with the social issues of the conflict and also because we believe that the military aspects (given their historical relevance) deserve to be explored to the same extent as the others, because ultimately they prove to be curious at the very least.

Finally, it's worth noting that in order to better understand the complexity of the Canudos War, it's essential to focus on the fact that in this conflict at the end of the 19th century there were two diametrically opposed forces: on the one hand, a professional military force and, on the other, ordinary people from the interior of the Bahian hinterland, simple residents of Canudos.

1 FROM THE MONARCHY TO REPUBLICAN BRAZIL

Before delving into the Canudos War with an emphasis on the military aspects of the combat and the decisions made by its military leaders, it is also essential to understand Brazil at the end of the 19th century, in particular the historical panorama and its institutions, and the socio-political movements that took place at the beginning of the Republic, including the insurrection in Canudos.

In this way, and with the aim of providing a better understanding of the proposed theme, but without losing sight of Sun Tzu's links in The Art of War, we have chosen to reinforce the aspects related to the study of History and the fact that this study should be correlated with stimulating curiosity to understand the world in which we live, and not just stimulating people to memorize chronological time and historical facts that happened on some date A or B.

For example, it's impossible to understand Modern Japan without studying the Meiji period in Japan. However, in the vast majority of history books I know, this is not mentioned at all, and it seems that Japanese history only began after the Second World War.

It is therefore necessary to encourage those interested in the study of history to get to know other cultures, or to understand the implications in a globalized scenario - even in the 19th century - of сото the formation and exercise of a particular culture and its repercussions in all spheres of society, why not, have repercussions on the History of Brazil itself.

As Sun Tzu shows us, the Art of War goes beyond the battlefield and can be seen in even the simplest day-to-day transformations.

No matter how critical the situation and circumstances in which you find yourself, don't despair. When everything inspires fear, you should fear nothing. When you are surrounded by every danger, you should fear none. When you have no recourse, you should rely on everyone. When you are surprised, surprise the enemy." (SUN TZU, 2000, p. 122)

And what dangers did the Brazilian state face at the end of the 19th century, and what fears might have haunted the still incipient Republic?

The proclamation of the Republic and its consolidation in the early years suffered from the most diverse influences, all coming from the different groups that worked for the Republic, but there was no single project for the Republic, but several, each seeking space in which to allocate their desires, rights and duties.

There was a positivist project, defended by the military, others sought a model based on the French Republic as a paradigm, in addition to the model defended by the farmers: a federalist republic, along the lines of the one implemented in the United States, because shortly before the Proclamation of the Republic and the fall of the Monarchy, the latter had made the end of slavery in Brazil official in one of its last acts.

In this turbulent scenario, the model of the Republic that prevailed was that of the landowners, expressed in the articles of the 1891 Constitution, even so, with antagonistic topics, reservations and disagreements, the result of concessions made in part by the authoritarian government of Marechai Deodoro.

Based on this tenuous structure created by the end of slavery (1888), the proclamation of the Republic (1889) and the new Constitution (1891), and also recalling the great positivist influence on the military then in power, it is worth quoting here the French philosopher Emile Durkheim, himself a member of the positivist school, who wisely explains in one sentence this explosive context that had formed in Brazil at the end of the 19th century:

Human passions only stop in the face of a moral force that they respect. If any such authority does not exist, it is the law of the strongest that reigns and, latent or acute, the state of war is necessarily chronic. (ALCANTARA, 2007, p. 123)

Since history is driven by collective and individual causes, and individual causes generally derive from human passions, the movements and insurrections of that period pitted segments of civil society and the armed forces against each other, defending different models of republican projects, but above all the interests of political, social, economic and even religious groups.

It's important to note that many of these movements didn't advocate or encourage the return of the Monarchy, but almost all of them yearned for change in the conduct of our incipient Republic, as we can see in the Canudos War there was an anti-republican component, but this wasn't the central cause of the Canudenses' resistance, but ended up being incorporated into the reality of the conflict as history unfolded.

From a social point of view, at the beginning of the Republic there was a huge mass of people excluded from the republican process, because a large part of the population that did not belong to the existing institutions or to the wealthier classes of society, was scarcely contemplated in the scenario of the Republic of 1889 and the Constitution of 1891.

This mass of excluded people didn't stop taking a stand, and during the Floriano Peixoto government in Rio de Janeiro, there was a lot of popular support for him, partly due to his actions against the high cost of living. This support came about through the creation of Jacobin clubs for volunteers to fight in the Federalist Revolution, which took place in the south of Brazil between 1893 and 1895.

It was then up to the first civilian president, Prudente de Moraes, to make a great effort to demobilize these popular contingents, who were also against civilian governments, and to face the years of war in Canudos between 1896 and 1897.

At the same time as the first decade of the Republic sought to strengthen a new democracy and proposed changes that would alter the republican framework, we can see that, as historian Emilia Viotti da Costa wrote, it is a very simplistic theory to think that only Marechai Deodoro da Fonseca was responsible for the proclamation of the Republic, in a symbolic and nationalistic act on the morning of November 15, 1889.

It is necessary to analyze the whole period at the end of the Second Reign, especially its socio-political and economic aspects, and sometimes even its cultural aspects, in order to understand the events that culminated in a revolutionary coup that led Brazil from a Monarchist model to a Republican model, because: "It is widely believed that the proclamation of the Republic resulted from the crises that shook the foundation of the Second Reign: the Religious Question, the Military Question and Abolition." (COSTA, 1998, p. 446).

It is also important to point out that "The portraits of the Monarchy and the Republican movement are diverse and contradictory." (COSTA,

1998, p. 450) and that they represented and were historically recorded according to the point of view of the figures participating in this moment in Brazilian history: Monarchists or Republicans.

It was only after more than 40 years of living in the republican environment, and with incentives from abroad - the 1929 crisis, and the transformations of a Brazil that was no longer purely agrarian - that new and more elaborate approaches emerged to the issue of identifying those truly responsible for the proclamation of the Republic, as the author states: "From 1930 onwards, when a new period in the country's political life was inaugurated, the history of the Republic came to be seen in an entirely new light." (COSTA, 1998, p. 451).

Also according to the author herself, and based on the transformations I mentioned in the 40-year period after November 15, 1899:

The proclamation of the Republic was therefore the result of profound transformations that had been taking place in the country. The decline of the traditional oligarchies, linked to land, abolition, immigration, the process of industrialization and urbanization, antagonism between producing areas, and the campaign for federation all contributed to undermining the monarchist edifice and sparking subversion. (COSTA, 1998, p. 451), and (...) sought to explain the movement as resulting from the inadequacy of the existing institutional framework to the new social and economic reality that had gradually taken hold in the country since 1870. (COSTA, 1998, p. 452).

There is no doubt that these statements by the author show that the economic power that emerged in the provinces was seeking greater space for political power in that period, meaning that "Abolition and the Republic are symptoms of the same reality; both are repercussions, at the institutional level, of changes that occurred in the country's economic structure that led to the destruction of traditional schemes." (COSTA, 1998, p. 455).

This also leads us to realize that Abolition has a fundamental link with the Republic, but even stronger with an attempt to preserve the Empire, because as the author states:

It should also be noted that Abolition only affected the sectors that remained attached to slave labor and these, in the 1880s, constituted the least dynamic part of the country, since the more progressive sectors were already preparing for the use of free labor. Only the farmers in the decadent, routine areas, who were unable to evolve to the new forms of production, remained attached to slave labor (COSTA, 1998, p. 455).

Clearly the beginning of the Republic benefited those who already lived off the favors of the Imperial state and who somehow needed to restructure themselves economically, using the factor of the loss of the slaves to search for possible compensation or forgiveness of their debts, since "During the long reign of Pedro II profound changes occurred in the Brazilian economy and society..." (COSTA, 1998, p. 463).

Given this scenario of economic transformations, and the innovative possibility of eliminating from the political field an imperial administration that, centralized in Rio de Janeiro, still had vestiges of an almost absolutist model versus the possibility represented by a federative ideal, it was clear that:

> Faced with so many contradictions, the solution seemed to lie in the federal system. The excessive centralization that characterized the imperial administration disgusted a portion of public opinion, which considered such a system an obstacle to the country's development and the solution of its most urgent problems. The idea of federation thus acquired greater prestige (COSTA, 1998, p. 470).

What was lacking was a model of force capable of leading these changes, and at the same time preserving the unity of the country, given that in many regions it was already being questioned whether there really was a national identity and "The separatist ideas were born out of the profound imbalance between political and economic power that was observed at the end of the empire, (...)" (COSTA, 1998, p. 472).

This model of force was glimpsed by the Republicans in the form of the army, which "(...) had already shown support for the abolitionist cause by refusing to chase runaway slaves. From then on, the military club was the main nucleus of the conspiracy. The Republic was thus born under the sign of the Army." (COSTA, 1998, p. 485).

In this way, it is not Marechai Deodoro da Fonseca, but the Army and the generalate of the military club in Rio de Janeiro who should receive responsibility, in the sense of execution, for the proclamation of the Republic, while in the sense of responsibility the patrons are in fact the combination and "(...) conjugation of three forces: one part of the army, farmers from the west of São Paulo and representatives of the urban middle classes who, in order to obtain their designs, indirectly relied on the discrediting of the monarchy and the weakening of the traditional oligarchies." (COSTA, 1998, p. 489).

Thus, in my view, it is not correct to attribute responsibility for the proclamation of the Republic to a single agent, but rather, as in all revolutions, to a series of internal and external factors that combined over many years to produce the maturity and opportunity for a transformative moment in Brazilian history that occurred on November 15, 1889.

But if politics, the economy and society were strengthened by the new role of the Army in the early years of the Republic, what was happening in the Catholic Church and what were the consequences?

The role of the Catholic Church in Brazilian society at the end of the 19th century was undergoing a political-institutional transition, as was the case with almost all the institutions existing at that time, whether in its internal organizational environment or externally in the way it dealt with its followers.

During the imperial period in Brazil, the State and the Church were deeply intertwined, but with the advent of the Republic in 1889, new winds of freedom of action were provided and these links between State and Church were broken, resulting in many complaints from ecclesiastical leaders.

This new panorama created a vacuum for the Church in some places, especially in the interior of Brazil, where the religious authorities found it more difficult to adapt to the new political limits imposed by the Republic.

As a result, popular religious movements of a mystical and profane nature (arising from the "mixing" of different native cultures with Christian dogmas) emerged and took hold.

These "messianic movements", or millenarian movements, in the form of their advisors, monks and friars, occupied the social and political spheres of this new scenario, and mobilized legions of devotees, such as the Juazeiro, Canudos and Contestado movements.

These three movements, each with completely different origins, objectives and socio-political aspects, violated the religiosity advocated by the Catholic Church insofar as they resulted from "(...) the colonizer's adjustment to the new world, either by transferring or modifying the traits of the original culture (...)" (HERMANN, 2013, p. 126).

In this way, religion was just one of the strongest expressions of the changes that the country was going through, and for Brazilians who lived far from the big centers it didn't seem to be clear how they worked, and the Church was part of this process, because until then it was, above all, a representative of the emperor's power in many parts of the country.

In addition, the Church in Rome sought to politically curb the prestige and power acquired by the followers of the messianic movements, as they ultimately represented a loss of influence and power on the part of the Catholic Church, and ultimately a reduction in the economic contribution received from the faithful, which weakened the Holy See's coffers.

This is most evident in the case of Juazeiro, where brotherhoods were created to support Padre Cicero, diverting resources that could have been channeled to the Holy See.

In Canudos, the threat was more doctrinal than economic, since abandoning the traditional rites of the Church and following "(...) superstitious doctrines and an excessively rigid morality that is disturbing consciences (...)" (HERMANN, 2013, p. 141) created a window of opportunity for the emergence of yet another dissent from the Catholic Church, as had occurred many centuries earlier in Europe with Luther and the origins of the Anglican Church.

In Contestado, the threat to the religiosity advocated by the Catholic Church came from an organization that "(...) mixed military preparations and religious ceremonies (...)" (HERMANN, 2013, p. 150), in a clear allusion to and similarity with movements already faced in the past by the Church in Europe сото о the Templars and other military-religious societies existing especially during the Middle Ages, and which in the future could once again threaten the already weakened power of the Church in Brazil.

As for the historiographical production on these three events dealt with in Jacqueline Hermann's text, the different interpretations can be divided into two broad lines of thought, where before l960 they were seen purely as movements of a religious nature, permeated with syncretism and/or fanaticism, and after l960 as movements of a political and social context, intensely related to the political changes in the country, the agrarian problems related to landlordism, the problems of integrating the new population contingents (freed blacks and European immigrants, in particular), and the great economic disparity between the regions, those where the movements took place and the large centers existing in Brazil at that time.

To illustrate this situation, let's take the example of Canudos where:

(...) at least two major interpretative strands can be clearly identified: the "Euclidean" one, derived from Euclides da Cunha's classic Os sertoes, and what I call the "progressive" one, which emerged in the 1960s and identified with the political issues of its time. (HERMANN, 2013, p. 138).

Specifically in the region of Canudos, in the interior of the Bahian sertao, coronelista practices and the politics of the governors still represented a rangoon acquired by Brazil in its origins and preserved сото hideous legacy, mainly from Brazil Imperio.

During the period of the Empire, and even before during the Colonial period and its hereditary captaincies, a model was always conceived in Brazil that was almost feudal, where the Lord of the Lands, or his representative, was the "owner of everything" and exercised power in every possible way, whether directly or indirectly, and affecting all spheres of society, whether in politics, economics, culture and sometimes even religion, thus creating a guarantee of continuity in power whatever the political model or form of government in force.

This model, and this form of power, is a clear offense and condemnation of any principle of citizenship and representativeness of society, because the citizen, being the weakest link in this process, ends up being subjected to and forced to agree with decisions that don't always, or worse, most of the time don't reflect or meet their most basic needs for life in society or their rights as a Brazilian. As a result, their only participatory link in the model (the vote) is subjugated by the exercise of power.

Although it seems disassociated from the Canudos War, and keeping in mind the social point of view of the Canudos War, it is important to note that the Vaccine Revolt took place a few years after the end of the Canudos War:

Rio de Janeiro was still a "den" of tropical diseases, such as yellow fever and variola. It was believed that the accumulation of people in small spaces was the cause of these diseases. The miserable people in the center of Rio de Janeiro were blamed by the authorities for spreading disease, violence and banditry. The elites believed that they should be removed from the area in order to transform it into a "clean" area, i.e. one suitable for the local bourgeoisie. The people who put this plan into practice were the mayor of Rio de Janeiro, Pereira Passos, and the president of Rio de Janeiro.

Republic, Rodrigues Alves, from 1901." (BURD, 2012).

From this text, it is clear that the Vaccine Revolt, like the Canudos War, also had a political and social connotation - it was an act of resistance to acts perpetrated by a few, but which affected a large section of the population, but this time in a large population center in Brazil at the time and not in some remote part of the country, as in the cases of Juazeiro, Canudos or Contestado.

It is also worth remembering that the first favelas appeared in Rio de Janeiro precisely because of the contingents of Army pests who returned from the Canudos War and had сото only option to live precisely in these agglomerations of people in the center of Rio de Janeiro. As Rafael Burd quotes:

Strictly speaking, it was a rebellion against the excesses committed by the authorities against a deprived and needy population. For many years, instead of help, this population had only been reprimanded and harmed. The vaccine was only the last straw, the immediate cause of the revolt. The project of the Republic implemented in 1889 was liberal from an economic point of view, authoritarian from a political point of view and exclusionary from a social point of view (BURD, 2012).

2 STRAWS

The episode of the Canudos War, although it has been documented dozens of times, is still one of the most interesting topics in Brazilian military historiography, and neither are the available archaeological details of the expeditions, their composition, their deeds, the itineraries, the fighting and the return of the troops exhausted, although, since the 1960s, studies have focused excessively on the social issues involved.

It's important to point out that several authors in Brazilian history and literature who have been to Canudos and written about the subject always start with the saga of Antonio Vicente Mendes Maciel - better known as Antonio Conselheiro - and his community of sertanejos, but they don't go into much detail about the military's operational characteristics.

Among these authors, who left aside the approach of those who were actually in combat and didn't explore the dexterity, capacity, employment and audacity of the Brazilian Army in resolving the situation that arose, even though they were soldiers in actual service during the conflict, we have: Henrique Duque-Estrada de Macedo Soares, Dantas Barreto, Manuel Benicio, Orvacio Deolindo da Cunha Marreca, and above all, Euclides da Cunha.

To illustrate this situation, of the different historiographical perspectives before and after l960, we can easily take the example of Canudos as a basis, because according to Hermann (2013, p. 138), "at least two major interpretative strands can be clearly identified: the 'Euclidean' one, derived from the classic The sertoes, by Euclides da

Cunha, and the one I call "progressive", which emerged in the 1960s and identified with the political issues of its time."

That said, in this paper we will explore the subject from a third angle, focusing mainly on the actions of the Brazilian Army and the military aspects of fighting the Canudos War:

> For some time, the works written by the military were repudiated, serving to prove their authoritarian and conservative thinking, but now with the new studies on Military History they are gaining more space and being re-read by authors such as Celso Castro and Jose Murilo de Carvalho, in search of the social profile of the military and the logic of the corporations. (GOMES FILHO, 2007, p. 7)

3 SUN TZU IN THE CANUDOS WAR

O terrain influences both the decisions related to strategy and the tactics that must be employed in the deployment of military forces.

Geography is essential for decision-making and the use of ground forces, especially with regard to the topography of the terrain, its covers and shelters, land and water routes, as well as its exploitability, as Sun Tzu teaches us:

The surface of the Earth has an infinite variety of places. You must flee from some and seek out others. However, you must know all the terrain perfectly. [...]. A well-prepared enemy, against whom your attack failed at the first onslaught, is dangerous. [...]. Assume, as a matter of principle, that your enemy is just as keen to gain an advantage as you are. Use all your arguments to deceive him. Above all, don't attack him directly. Remember that there are different ways of deceiving and being deceived (SUN TZU, 2000, p. 101-112).

The Canudos area is located to the north of Salvador, in the interior of the Bahian hinterland, delimited by five mountain ranges (Canabrava, Cocorobo, Calumbi, Cambaio and Acipa) and with a river called Vaza Barris at its center. It is an arid region, with typical poor and thorny caatinga vegetation, with a predominantly dry climate, which often leaves it exposed to long periods of drought.

Allied to this scenario, the complete omission of the state at the end of the 19th century provided Antonio Conselheiro with the perfect conditions to establish a community in this place made up of individuals forgotten by the authorities who resided in the major centers of the republic. In the Military History II: Republican Period handout for Unisul's Military History specialization course, the occupation of the Canudos region during that period is described as follows:

In the region, there were a few small, decaying villages with rustic wattle and daub houses and a population that was mostly miserable, ignorant and superstitious, living in a semi-feudal society dominated by the coroneis, under the influence of a rustic, rural, Sebastianist messianism. (UNISUL, 2010, p. 65)

A 1ª . Expedigao - Lieutenant Manoel da Silva Pires Ferreira

The small community of Canudos, hitherto made up of individuals forgotten by society and the state, grew dramatically with the arrival of Antonio Conselheiro, becoming a regional threat to the economic status quo of the colonizers and, consequently, of the state itself:

The village's economy was based on the production and sale of leather from goats that were raised in the caatinga. In the short term, Canudos became an attraction for sertanejos in search of hope, fugitives from justice, deserters and bandits. It is estimated to have had between 25,000 and 30,000 inhabitants, living in around 5,400 houses. They could have mobilized 5,000 men-at-arms (UNISUL, 2010, p. 66).

In 1896, the threat to the state seemed to become evident when 44 soldiers from the Bahia Police Force were killed by Canudenses in the Massete region, after a disagreement with timber merchants from Juazeiro, because the residents of Canudos had bought and paid for the timber, but the Juazeiro merchants refused to deliver it.

At this point, the judge of law in Juazeiro asked the President of the State of Bahia for support, who in turn asked General Solon Ribeiro - Commander of the 3rd Military District - to send a hundred soldiers to the region. Military District - to send a hundred soldiers to the region.

O General Solon Ribeiro, having under his command the 9th Infantry Battalion, based in Salvador, also received direct orders from General

Dionisio Cerqueira to deploy his staff, at which point he was warned by Colonel Tamarindo - Commander of the 9th Infantry Battalion - that "Canudos would be a bomb exploding in the hands of the Army." (UNISUL, 2010, p. 67).

So, in order to comply with what he had been ordered to do, General Solon Ribeiro ordered Lieutenant Manoel da Silva Pires Ferreira to travel to Juazeiro, taking with him an infantry unit made up of three officers and 104 squads, which would later be reinforced with a medical officer, an ambulance and its staff, canisters of material and medicines.

Beginning the 1ª . Expedition to Canudos, Lieutenant Pires Ferreira led his troops to Juazeiro by rail.

Lieutenant Pires Ferreira's staff, in addition to being small, poorly armed, poorly trained, poorly dressed - in trousers and the unit's uniform - in other words, without adequate equipment for the operation to be carried out, was made up mostly of poorly educated and physically unprepared men, and not enough of all these problems, it still didn't have the appropriate logistical support, which would have been provided by the local authorities.

The logistical limitations and unpreparedness of this operation were such that the troops didn't even have tents. Worse still, nothing had been defined about the mission to be carried out by Lieutenant Pires Ferreira, not even about the limits of the troop's action.

Once in Juazeiro, where he arrived on November 7, 1896, Lieutenant Pires Ferreira was coerced by the local authorities into attacking Canudos.

Thus, although he was aware of his operational limitations, he headed for the small town of Uaua in order to reconnoiter the area, because not only did he not have detailed information about the enemy, but his men still suffered from the lack of any kind of logistics (water, food and even ammunition).

As we can see from Sun Tzu's teachings, by giving in to this coercion from the political forces of Juazeiro, Lieutenant Pires Ferreira ran a risk that apparently had not been well calculated or mitigated.

If you're inferior, stay alert - the slightest mistake could be fatal. Try to keep yourself safe, and avoid clashing with your opponent if possible. The prudence and firmness of a handful of people can extenuate and dominate even a large army. In this way, you are both able to protect yourself and achieve a complete victory. (SUN TZU, 2000, p. 37)

The town of Uaua was located to the west of Canudos, on the banks of the River Vaza Barris, approximately 192 kilometers away.

Arriving in Uaua on November 19, 1896, Lieutenant Pires Ferreira found the village abandoned. Faced with this situation and the fact that it had no tents, and realizing how exhausted his men were, Lieutenant Pires Ferreira ordered the troops to carry out a bivouac, but without first organizing the security of the place.

Soon, aware of the presence of army troops in Uaua, Antonio Conselheiro's Canudenses began to unsettle the troops through guerrilla techniques.

The situation progressed to conflict when the troops were directly attacked by the Canudenses at five o'clock on November 21. During the confrontation, the Canudenses occupied the empty houses, to the same extent as the army troops, but with a delay in forming and organizing an effective defence, due to their low level of preparation and operational training.

In the course of the conflict, an army soldier is imprisoned and beheaded by the Canudenses, prompting Lieutenant Pires Ferreira to order the houses occupied by the Canudenses to be set on fire in order to force them out into open combat.

This order was followed by fierce fighting, which lasted four hours, until the Canudenses decided to withdraw to Canudos, much to the good fortune of the army troops, who were practically out of ammunition. Thanks to their superior weaponry, the troops were able to repel the attack by carrying out a mass shooting and causing the deaths of approximately 150 Canudenses.

Finally, Lieutenant Pires Ferreira's troops remained in Uaua for one more night and began their retreat to Juazeiro on November 22, but with 10 dead and 17 wounded in combat, in the episode of the 40th Army District in the state of Rio de Janeiro.

the previous day. Although in his report Lieutenant Pires Ferreira estimates that he was attacked by around three thousand Canudenses, more recent sources estimate the number at between 500 and 1,100 men.

Table 1 - Troops involved in the 1ª . Expedition to Canudos

TROOPS	**Battle of Uaua**	
	Army	**Canudenses**
In combat	-150	500 - 1.100
Dead	10	-150
Injured	17	N/A

Source: Author (2017).

A 2ª . Expedigao - Major Febronio de Brito

Lieutenant Pires Ferreira's return to Juazeiro caused great concern, alarming the President of the State and the Commander of the Military District.

In November 1896, General Solon Ribeiro decided to immediately organize a second expedition to Canudos, again under the political influence of General Dionisio Cerqueira (interim сото Minister of War) and after being pressured by Luiz Viana (President of the State of Bahia) to come up with a quick solution to the situation, without, however, providing the necessary resources for such an undertaking.

This new expedition against Canudos was organized without the proper operational links having been learned, especially those relating to logistics and knowledge of the terrain's topography, which should have been obtained from the results of the first expedition.

In this way, once again, the military leadership of the Brazilian Army, yielding to regional political pressures, ignored the "science of the art of war" and relegated the necessary preparations for the combat that was on the horizon to second place, as Sun Tzu points out:

Aware of your abilities and limitations, don't start any endeavor that you can't complete. Decipher far and near with the same skill, so that what unfolds before your eyes is identical to what lies beyond them. (SUN TZU, 2000, p. 24)

[a]In order to mitigate the lack of knowledge of the terrain and the logistical problems, the troops of the 2nd Expedition were equipped with greater firepower, receiving reinforcements of four Nordenfelt machine guns, two Krupp Cal 8 cannons, a small garrison and some ammunition.

Against this backdrop, the 2ª . Expedition to Canudos, under the command of Major Febronio de Brito, who inexplicably received direct orders from the Governor. This 2ª . Expedition would be made up of members of the Brazilian Army, men from the Bahia Police Force and bureaucrats not prepared for combat. Reinforcements, in terms of men and ammunition, would be provided by the states of Alagoas and Sergipe.

On November 25, 1896, the 2ª . Expedition left for the town of Queimadas, located to the south of the city of Monte Santo. Arriving there on the 26th, Major Febronio de Brito immediately informed General Solon Ribeiro of his difficulties, the main one being the lack of information about the enemy.

On December 7, believing rumors about Antonio Conselheiro and the operational capacity of his Canudenses in combat, Major Febronio de Brito telegraphed General Solon Ribeiro that it would be possible to attack Canudos as long as he had around five hundred armed men.

Having done so, he suddenly and inexplicably moved his men to Monte Santo, in the direction of Canudos.

With regard to this fact, here's another link from Sun Tzu:

Know your enemy and know yourself; if you have a hundred fights to fight, a hundred times you will be victorious. If you ignore your enemy and know yourself, your chances of losing and winning will be the same. If you ignore both your enemy and yourself, you will only count your battles as defeats. (SUN TZU, 2000, p. 41)

Major Febronio de Brito made a hasty decision without the consent of General Solon Ribeiro, who ordered him to immediately return to Queimadas, as he believed there was a need for a larger contingent. On the other hand, Luiz Viana, sharing the same opinion as Major Febronio de Brito, believes that an additional hundred men would be sufficient for the task.

ªThis operational disagreement between General Solon Ribeiro and Luiz Viana was followed by other political disagreements - for example, over who would be responsible for maintaining public order in the state - which led Viana to withdraw the 100 men of the Bahia Police Force from the 2nd Expedition, ordering them to go alone to Monte Santo under the command of a Captain.

These political impasses were followed by others that culminated in General Solon Ribeiro's removal from command of the 3rd Military District and his replacement by Colonel Saturnino Ribeiro da Costa Junior. He was replaced by Colonel Saturnino Ribeiro da Costa Junior, who went on to fulfill Luiz Viana's wishes, while neglecting the military aspects of preparing the operation, especially with regard to information.

Thus, with approximately 550 men in the 2ª . Major Febronio de Brito set off from Monte Santo towards Canudos, reaching the region of the Cambaio and Caipan mountains without incident. From this point, on January 16, 1897, he entrenched himself near the outer area of Canudos.

On January 18, 1897, the Infantry moved towards Canudos under the fire support of the Artillery, equipped with Krupp cannons.

After five hours of combat, without managing to gain any ground, Major Febronio opted to divide the infantry into two columns, launching a direct attack on the enemy positions, followed by bayonet fighting.

[a]This maneuver, although effective, resulted in four dead and fifteen wounded, leading the troops of the 2nd Expedition to camp that night just six kilometers from Canudos and displacing the Canudenses to a second line of defense.

On January 19, 1897, the infantry began moving towards Canudos, but was surprised by a violent attack from the Canudenses. After some initial indecision and panic because the Canudenses were trying to seize the artillery emplacements, there followed an energetic reaction in combat by the army troops.

At the end of that day, and despite the initial success, Major Febronio de Brito ordered the withdrawal of the troops under his command, claiming that there were no conditions for them to remain in combat given the disproportionate number of troops between the Army and the Canudenses, and the exiguous amount of water and food, forcing his men to make the painful 104-kilometer return to Monte Santo.

Table 2 - Troops involved in the 2ª . Expedition to Canudos

TROOPS	**Battle of Uaua**	
	Army	**Canudenses**
In combat	-550	- 4.000
Dead	6	-700
Injured	20	N/A

Source: Author (2017).

A 3ª . Expedigao - Colonel Antonio Moreira Cesar

The arrival of the army troops in Monte Santo, again defeated in Canudos, raised even greater political and institutional alarm in the capital of the Republic, Rio de Janeiro.

The victory of the conselheiristas helped create a mystique of invincibility in relation to Canudos. Many sertanejos flocked there, considering the place impregnable and protected by God. In the Federal Capital, military authorities began to accuse the government of being unable to quell the "monarchist uprising". (FARIA, 2015, p.213)

ªWith the defeat of the 2nd Expedition and the consequent increase in political pressure caused by public opinion, the negative repercussions of the failure of the first two expeditions were felt in the Federal Capital.

As a result, the Brazilian army and the local authorities in Bahia, once again forced to hastily prepare a new expedition, did so in a disastrous way, relegating to second place, as in previous expeditions, fundamental factors related to logistics, detailed information about the enemy and the terrain where the troops would be operating.

ªThe command of the 3rd Expedition was defined directly by the President in office (Manoel Vitorino) and assigned to Infantry Colonel Antonio Moreira Cesar, with Colonel Pedro Nunes Batista Ferreira Tamarindo, from the 9th Infantry Battalion in Salvador, as deputy commander.

O Colonel Moreira Cesar, a military man experienced in combat, having played an important role in the recent Federalist Revolution (1893 - 1895) сото Military Governor of Santa Catarina, and due to his history in this conflict, he was considered сото a cold and calculating man.

In Santa Catarina, Colonel Moreira Cesar became known as a military man "(...) temperamental, ambitious, determined, brave and polemical. His performance during the Federalist Revolution, on the island of Desterro, has been criticized to this day because of the arrests and shootings that took place. He was also a sick man." (UNISUL, 2010, p. 74).

Given the turbulent political climate, in which political influences hindered the planning and execution of military operations in the Sertao of Bahia, Colonel Moreira Cesar seemed to have the ideal profile for the job.

So the 3ª . Expedition was set up as "a brigade with 1,330 men from the 7th, 9th and 16th Infantry Battalions, plus a battery of Krupp L24 guns (4 pegs), a cavalry squad and members of the Bahian Military Police. Infantry Battalions, plus a battery of Krupp L24 guns (4 handles), a cavalry squadron and elements of the Bahian Military Police." (UNISUL, 2010, p. 75).

O Colonel Moreira Cesar arrived in Salvador on February 8 and left the following day for Queimadas, south of Monte Santo, to meet the troops in preparation.

Like his predecessors, he doesn't worry about the information available (especially the reports of the first two expeditions), but he soon realizes the problems related to logistical support, since he depends on the already scarce resources that were shared with the local population.

On February 17, 1897, the 3ª . The expedition headed for Monte Santo, only arriving there after five days, due to the epileptic seizure suffered by Colonel Moreira Cesar during the journey.

Having overcome this unforeseen event, the expedition set off in an easterly direction, to Cumbe, this time avoiding the places where Major Febronio de Brito had been ambushed during the 2ª . Expedition.

In the meantime, although Colonel Moreira Cesar was once again suffering from an epileptic seizure, the officers of his General Staff did not give him any recommendations, and the 3ª . The expedition continued north to the town of Rancho do Vigario, in the Serra do Aracary, arriving there on March 2.

The troops continued north, reaching the Pitombas region, where for the first time they encountered resistance from the Canudenses. On this occasion, the "7th. Battalion, which was in the vanguard, moved into position, received artillery support by hitting the main points of the enemy position and launched a bayonet attack, dislodging the Canudenses from their trenches. The march continued to Angico." (UNISUL, 2010, p. 76).

On reaching Angico, Colonel Moreira Cesar decided suddenly and without any rest for the troops: "let's go to Canudos for lunch" (UNISUL, 2010, p. 76). Sun Tzu, when discussing the "Art of Mudangas", warns of the need to guard against what he calls five defects, apparently innocuous, but which jeopardize the whole strategy, citing enthusiasm as the first of them:

The first is the excessive enthusiasm for facing death, a reckless attitude that honors itself as "courage", "intrepidity" and "valor", but, in essence, only deserves to be called "cowardice". A General who exposes himself unnecessarily, as if he were a simple soldier, who seems to seek the dangers of death, who fights and orders combat to the limit, is a man who deserves to die. He's a rash man, incapable of finding the resources to get out of a bad moment. He is a coward, incapable of suffering the slightest setback without becoming frustrated, believing that all is lost if he doesn't go exactly according to plan. (SUN TZU, 2000, p. 84)

Could this be a foretaste of what would happen with the 3rd Expedition?

Apparently so.

Thus, the troops set off on the attack on the afternoon of March 3rd, and it was decided that the 7th and 16th Infantry Battalions would take the right flank. Infantry Battalions would take the left flank, while the 9th Infantry Battalion plus the Bahia Police Force would take the right flank, and the Cavalry would cover the access road.

The artillery assaulted the fire zone for two hours, preparing the ground for the infantry's advance. The Infantry then launched a bayonet attack on the Canudenses entrenched in Canudos.

Although effective at first, the attack loses momentum as logistical problems resurface, leading to a lack of ammunition, as occurred in the first two expeditions.

Then, approximately five hours after the start of the fighting, Colonel Moreira Cesar was wounded in the belly as he prepared to go to the front to encourage the troops. [a]As soon as he was treated by the doctors, who found that he had been mortally wounded, command of the 3rd Expedition passed to Colonel Tamarindo.

Colonel Tamarindo, however, was unable to effectively take command and control of the troops deployed in the field.

Consequently, at 7 p.m. on March 3, he ordered the retreat to Fazenda Velha, from where, meeting with his General Staff, he decided to withdraw completely to Monte Santo, but with the artillery remaining in combat position to cover the evacuation of the wounded and the troops still operational.

Despite being against this withdrawal and insisting on a new attack, Colonel Moreira Cesar died at the age of 46, in the early hours of the morning of the *4th. At* six o'clock on the same day, the troops began to withdraw. However, at around eight o'clock, it was suddenly attacked by the Canudenses, who pursued and killed as many soldiers as they could.

As a result, practically all the artillery troops were killed by the cannons, while the infantry and cavalry retreated in disarray towards Cumbe and Monte Santo, abandoning their weapons, wounded and even their clothes. Once again, we must remember what Sun Tzu tells us.

It plunges the adversary into inextricable trials and prolongs his exhaustion by keeping you at a distance. (SUN TZU, 2000, p. 25)

In the end, in this disastrous retreat, Colonel Tamarindo, Captain Jose Agostinho Salomao da Rocha (commander of the artillery) and many wounded soldiers and stragglers who couldn't get away quickly died.

Table 3 - Troops involved in the 3ª Expedition to Canudos

TROOPS	Battle of Uaua	
	Army	Jagungos
In combat	1330	N/A
Dead	-550	N/A
Injured	120	N/A

Source: Author (2017).

A 4a . Expedigao - General Artur Oscar de Andrade Guimaraes

The withdrawal of the 3a . Expedition can be considered one of the greatest disasters in the history of the Brazilian Army, since the defeat and the stampede were not enough, the troops were forced to travel around 200 kilometers between Canudos and Monte Santo, under pressure from the terror of new attacks by the Canudenses.

In April 1897, the news of yet another defeat for the federal troops resonated intensely in Rio de Janeiro. The third defeat sparked demonstrations calling for measures to destroy Canudos.

These demonstrations culminated in the destruction of three newspaper offices, all with monarchist tendencies, because it is important to remember that Brazil was still in the early years of the Republic and there was great concern about movements that could also be seen as an affront to the new form of organization of the Brazilian state.

In this climate of tension, the 4ª Expedition was organized in April, prepared by the then Minister of War, Marechai Carlos Machado de Bittencourt, and under the command of General Artur Oscar de Andrade Guimaraes.

This expedition was made up of two columns, commanded by Generals Joao da Silva Barbosa and Claudio do Amaral Savaget, each with more than four thousand soldiers equipped with the most modern weapons of the time.

As soon as the 4ª . Expedition began, military forces converged from all over Brazil on the states of Bahia and Sergipe, with Queimadas and Aracaju being the concentration points for troops in these states, respectively. The town of Monte Santo, in the interior of Bahia and close to Canudos, also began to receive men for the 4ª Expedition.

With the arrival in Monte Santo of the main officers and the Commander-in-Chief, the orders for the attack on Canudos were announced, with the division of the troops into two columns, and it was decided that they would leave from different places: Queimadas and Aracaju. However, this time the mistakes of previous expeditions would not be repeated.

Thus, before going on to Canudos, Queimadas was transformed into a training camp, since in addition to the need to train - due to the fact that the troops were poorly trained - there was also the need to organize logistical support, to clothe and supply the soldiers because, to make matters worse, the units' manpower was depleted, with many damaged weapons and incomplete equipment.

Once the most basic problems of the units had been resolved, the first column was formed with the personnel of the 1ª ., 2ª . and 3ª . Brigades, under the command of General Joao da Silva Barbosa, and the second column was formed by the 4ª ., 5ª . and 6ª . Brigades. Brigade, commanded by General Claudio do Amaral Savaget.

Thus defined, the two columns began their march towards Canudos from Monte Santo, with the first column advancing from the south and the second column from the east, coming from Aracaju.

Although the weak resistance encountered during the advance of the first column did not prevent the troops from marching, the movement of he force as a whole had problems with the fractioning of units and the logistics of the Infantry and Artillery ammunition convoys, which constantly strayed into the rear and sometimes got lost.

ªWhile the two columns organized their forces to maintain the advance against Canudos, on the Canudo side, the armaments obtained from the defeat of the 3rd Expedition helped with the defences they could create. In this way, the Canudenses sought to create defensive formations on the roads and at points where columns could advance, especially the second column, which was coming from the east.

The second column, commanded by General Savaget, had set out from Aracaju on May 22, 1897 and followed the Vaza Barris river, under the direct observation of the enemy. This column carried few supplies and no convoy in its rear, in order to speed up its movement.

The column replenished its supplies along the way, with food for the troops and fodder for the animals being obtained through supply contracts.

Meanwhile, the troops of the first column, coming from the south and commanded by General Silva Barbosa, arrived at Rancho do Vigario on May 24, 1897, already suffering from a lack of supplies and ammunition, due to the delay of the supply train brought by the 5th. Bahia Police Corps, which was under attack from the Canudenses.

When the first column was about 18 kilometers away from Canudos, it came up against the resistance of the Canudenses, and the first battle began. It was a quick fight that lasted about an hour, with few casualties on the Canudos side and, on the Brazilian Army side, one dead and two wounded.

[a]After the fight, the troops of the first column resumed their movement, passing the town of Pitombas, the site of the massacre of the 3rd Expedition, where the Canudenses had left the bodies of the dead from that fight in the open.

The progression of the first column continues until it reaches the top of Favela, the outermost area of Canudos, where it receives its worst attack yet.

The Canudenses, once again demonstrating their empirical knowledge of exploring the terrain and using the surprise effect, entrenched themselves close to the first column, causing the first column to enter the fight early in the morning after an overnight stay at the top of the Favela.

At this point, another operational error occurred, when the commander of one of the brigades (Colonel Flores) invested in a direct charge against the defenses of Canudos, exposing the troops to constant fire.

This assault attempt, which was totally reckless both because of the situation at the time and the way it was carried out - a typical direct strategy action that had already been used unsuccessfully on previous expeditions - led to him being shot and dying on the spot.

At the end of the day, with the resistance of the entrenched Canudenses, the exhaustion of the artillery projectiles and the infantry dependent on collecting ammunition from the dead soldiers, and facing the imminent risk of another disaster, the officers of the first column had no choice but to request help from the second column, which at that moment was preparing to attack Canudos.

The second column, which had reached the outskirts of Canudos on June 27, 1897, began its preparations for the final attack on Canudos the following day.

However, at around eight o'clock in the morning, when Savaget's division was ready for the attack, the General received news of the first column's request for help.

At this point, the attack on Canudos was aborted and the second column left to help the first.

Thanks to the help of Savaget's division, the first column doesn't meet with total disaster and the expedition completely collapses.

So the assault pianos are abandoned, the two columns reunited and the 5th[a] . Brigade sent by the expedition command to assist the detachment of the 5th. Bahia Police Corps, in order to recover part of the supply convoy, which at that point had already been partly taken by the Canudenses.

How regrettable it is to risk everything in a single combat, neglecting the winning strategy, and making the fate of your weapons depend on a single battle! (SUN TZU, 2000, p. 25)

The troops under the command of General Artur Oscar ended up camped at the top of the Favela and, once again, logistical difficulties and the problems they caused prevented them from advancing against Canudos.

In addition, the decision to remain on top of the Favela and begin the siege of the place, allows the Canudenses to put uninterrupted pressure on the soldiers sustaining the siege, causing unrest in the camp day and night, and often injuring someone.

According to Sun Tzu, the tactic of provoking enemy action that leads to exhaustion, either by cutting off supplies or by indirect action maneuvers, forces the enemy to wear themselves out in response to small isolated actions, or even to fight for food or water:

So, if the enemy is rested, you can tire him out; if he's well fed, you can starve him; if he's resting, you can move him. Advance to the positions he needs to run to. Run where he doesn't expect you to (SUN TZU, 2000, p. 82).

The situation didn't improve until July 13, 1897, with the arrival of a convoy with food which, although scarce (enough for two or three days), was still enough to give the troops a new lease of life. With this reinforcement of food and ammunition, the force under the command of Artur Oscar prepared a new offensive for July 18th, starting from Favela, but it failed again.

The failure of the July 18 attack once again triggered dramatic logistical problems and the need to send in reinforcements to make up for the casualties in the units. Sun Tzu advocated this:

If you find yourself in a field of death, seek combat. I call those places of death where there are no resources, where the air is inescapably unhealthy, where provisions are dwindling with no hope of being replenished; where diseases are beginning to spread in the army, foreshadowing great scourges. If you find yourself in such circumstances, rush into battle. I assure you that your troops will be quick to fight. Dying at the hand of the enemy will seem mild to them compared to all the evils that torment them (SUN TZU, 2000, p. 78-79).

The expansion and availability of the available troops resulted in a new offensive on September 7, followed by another on September 11, in which the expeditionary troops took the hill next to Fazenda Velha and cut off communication with the Canudenses through that position.

A few days later, on September 24th, the siege was completed with the seizure of the land leading to the road to Uaua and the conflict continued with the siege moving towards the interior of the 6th district.locality and breaking the resistance of the Canudenses with constant attacks.

On October 2, after intense artillery fire the previous day, the expeditionary forces advanced into the interior of Canudos, and although they made a strong infantry attack against the Canudenses, the Brazilian army troops were repelled with intensity.

This violent confrontation continued for two more days, with intense attacks on the defenses of Canudos, creating a scene of total destruction and leaving thousands of bodies decomposing in the open.

Finally, on October 5, 1897, Canudos had its final end, when the commanders of the expeditionary forces were informed of the death of its last defenders.

Table 4 - Troops involved in the 4ª Expedition to Canudos

TROOPS	Battle of Uaua	
	Army	**Canudenses**
In combat	- 10.300	-25.000
Dead	- 2.500	- 20.000
Injured	N/A	N/A

Source: Author (2017).

4 CONCLUSIONS

The Canudos War played an important role in the changes that took place in the strategic, tactical and operational military thinking of the Brazilian Army's military leaders at the end of the 19th century.

At that time, the conflict gained notoriety and mobilized society, increasing the popular outcry for the closure of Canudos after the failure of the third expedition, because with the appeal of the press, the government was forced to mobilize approximately twelve thousand soldiers from seventeen Brazilian states, to end an internal conflict that had been going on for almost two years.

From that moment on, the Canudos War took on the characteristics of an "absolute war" in its last expedition, a war that sought the complete defeat and destruction of Canudos.

Since the beginning of the conflict, it has been clear that military power has been expanded and improved with each expedition, both in terms of personnel and military equipment.

It is important to note that the increase in the number of personnel and equipment of the expeditionary forces in the Sertao of Bahia required logistical support provided by bases of operations located in the towns of Queimadas and Monte Santo, as well as the establishment of lines of communication (by telegraph) and transportation (by rail), something hitherto unheard of in the Brazilian army.

In contrast to this increase in military power, the Canudese leadership apparently practiced Sun Tzu's knowledge empirically, making constant use of the resources of dissimulation:

Every military campaign is based on dissimulation. Pretend disorder. Never fail to offer the enemy a bait to deceive him. Simulate inferiority to encourage arrogance. Stir up his anger to better plunge him into confusion. His cowardice will hurl itself at you and then he will shatter." (SUN TZU, 2000, p. 25)

Thus, although the expeditionary forces had far greater military power than the Canudenses, the latter, using guerrilla tactics and dissimulation, managed to resist the Federal Government's offensives, and Canudos was only turned into ashes by the arson attacks at the end of the conflict.

It should be noted that the destruction of Canudos took place not only from a material point of view, but also from a human one, since it culminated in a confrontation that resulted in the deaths of more than 25,000 people.

So, from all that has been said so far, we can conclude that although military power is fundamental, the strategy factor should never be relegated to second place.

As Sun Tzu teaches us, military strategy is of the utmost importance for the constitutional preservation of a nation:

War is of crucial importance to the state. It is the realm of life and death. The preservation or ruin of the empire depends on it. Those of us who seriously reflect on the subject show a reprehensible indifference to the preservation or loss of what we hold most dear. (SUN TZU, 2000, p. 20)

The Canudos War was directly responsible for the transformations that took place in the army at the beginning of the 20th century, especially with regard to European-style Direct Strategies, which proved to be inefficient and ineffective in a conflict with the peculiarities of the Brazilian interior.

5 REFERENCE WORKS

ALCANTARA, Fernanda Henrique Cupertino. **The classics in everyday life.** Sao Paulo: arte & Ciencia, 2007.

BURD, Rafael. O **bota abaixo and the Vaccine Revolt.** 2012. Available at: <http://historiaeavida.blogspot.com/2012/02/o-bota-abaixo-e-revolta-da-vacina.html>. Accessed on: Aug. 19, 2018.

CLAUSEWITZ, Carl Von. **On war.** 1984. Translated by the Brazilian Naval War College, CMG (RRm) Luiz Carlos Nascimento e Silva do Valle. Available at: <https://www.egn.mar.mil.br/arquivos/cepe/DAGUERRA.pdf>. Accessed on: June 18, 2017.

COSTA, Emilia Viotti da. **From the Monarchy to the Republic, decisive moments.** Chapter 11. Editora UNESP, 1998.

FARIA, Durland Puppin. **Introduction to Brazilian Military History.** Resende: Academia Militar das Agulhas Negras, 2015. Available at: <http://www.cporpa.eb.mil.br/images/2016/int/hist_mil/UDIV/Apostila_Historia_Militar_Brasileira_Cap_6.pdf>. Accessed on: May 25, 2017.

HERMANN, Jacqueline. **Religion and politics at the dawn of the Republic: the movements of Juazeiro, Canudos and Contestado.** In: FERREIRA, Jorge; DELGADO, Lucilia deA. N. O **Republican Brazil.** Volume 1: The time of exclusionary liberalism. From the proclamation of the Republic to the 1930 Revolution. 6ª edition. Rio de Janeiro: Civilizagao Brasileira, 2013.

FGV CPDOC. **Infographics of expedition numbers and casualties against Canudos.** Available at <http://atlas.fgv.br/marcos/anos-de-incerteza/mapas/efetivos-e-baixas-das-expedicoes-contra-canudos>. Accessed on June 28, 2017.

GOMES FILHO, Gregorio Ferreira. **Shadows of Brazilian historiography: Marreca and the Para military regiment in Canudos.** Federal University of Roraima. Paper presented at the IV History Week of the Federal University of Roraima, October 9-11, 2007. Available at: < http://revista.ufrr.br/examapaku/article/view/1458>. Accessed on: 08jun. 2017.

MCCANN, Frank D. **Soldados da patria: Historia do Exercito Brasileiro 1889-1937.** 1 ed. Rio de Janeiro: Biblioteca do Exercito Editora, 2009.

MELLO, Frederico Pernambucano de. **The total war of Canudos.** 3rd Edition, Sao Paulo: Escrituras Editora, 2014.

RESENDE, Maria Efigenia Lage de. O **process© politico na Primeira Republica e o liberalism© oligarquico.** In: FERREIRA, Jorge; DELGADO, Lucilia de A. N. O **Brasil republican©.** Volume 1: The time of exclusionary liberalism. From the proclamation of the Republic to the 1930 Revolution. 6ª edition. Rio de Janeiro: Civilizagao Brasileira, 2013.

SANTACREU, Gabriel. Sun **Tzu has never been so current.** Meio&mensagem. Published on April 12, 2017. Available at: < http://www.meioemensagem.com.br/home/opiniao/2017/04/12/sun-tzu-nunca-foi-tao-atual.html>. Accessed on: August 27, 2018.

SUN TZU. **The Art of War.** Translated from Chinese into French by Father Amiot in 1772, and into Portuguese by CASSAL, Sueli Barros. 1st edition. Porto Alegre: L&PM Editores, 2000.

THE GIVER. Direction: Phillip Noyce. Produced by: Neil Koenigsberg; Nikki Silver. Performers: Jeff Bridges; Meryl Streep; Katie Holmes; Taylor Swift and others. Screenplay: Michael Mitnick. Music: Marco Beltrami. 97min. Los Angeles: Walden Media, 2014.

UNISUL, Textbook. **Brazilian Military History II: republican period.** Palhoga-SC: UnisulVirtual, 2010.

Printed by Books on Demand GmbH, Norderstedt / Germany